Working With
Clay and Plaster

Working With
Clay and Plaster

David Cowley

B T Batsford Limited   London
Watson-Guptill Publications   New York

Copyright © David Cowley 1973
First published 1973
ISBN 0 7134 2309 9

Library of Congress Cataloging
in Publication Data

Cowley, David
Working with Clay and Plaster
Bibliography: p
1   Plaster casts.   2   Clay.   3   Modeling.   1   Title
TT295.C68   1973   731.4   72–10024
ISBN 0–8230–5866–2

Filmset by Keyspools Limited, Golborne, Lancashire
Printed in Great Britain by
The Anchor Press Limited, Tiptree, Essex
Bound by William Brendon and Son Limited
Tiptree, Essex
for the publishers
B T Batsford Limited
4 Fitzhardinge Street, London W1H 0AH and
Watson-Guptill Publications
1515 Broadway, New York, NY 10036

Contents

Acknowledgment

I wish to thank the following who have helped in the preparation of this book: Jyl Cowley and the pupils of Eltham Green School; the students of Whitelands College; and Nichola, Janine and Colin Youngs.

I am especially grateful to Tony Youles who took most of the photographs, to Ray Youngs for figures 1, 43, 113, 114, 115, 116 and 117, to Nicos Moshatos for figures 79, 80 and 81, and to Nick Tweddell for figures 40, 41 and 42.

Finally I would like to thank Phyllis Fountain, Nora Proud and Thelma M. Nye who have patiently given much encouragement and invaluable critical and clerical help.

London 1973   DC

7

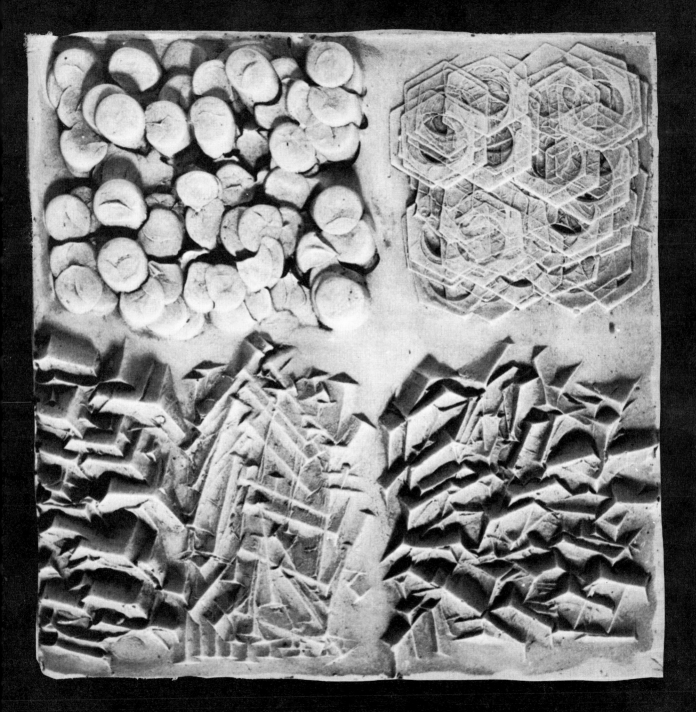

Introduction

A direct and simple approach to casting in plaster from a clay mould can provide the basis for much valuable and interesting creative work by children and adults. The process, as the illustrations will show, can be used in a variety of ways in the classroom and in the home, with a minimum of cost, equipment, and previous experience.

Plaster casting is often associated with complicated techniques used by sculptors—which are certainly not suitable for young children, large classes in schools, or the inexperienced adult. However, the process is basically a method of achieving a positive form from a negative mould: a finger pressed deeply into a pliable material such as clay will leave an impression, or a negative. When liquid plaster poured into this 'mould' has set and is separated from the soft clay, it forms the positive or 'cast'. This should be an exact plaster replica of the finger, or whatever was pressed into the clay.

This simple technique is explored in the following pages. Within the framework of the methods described there are limitless possibilities for creative work by adults and children, irrespective of their age or ability.

Materials and equipment

Two materials are essential: clay, out of which the mould is made, and plaster, which is used to fill the mould and to produce the cast. Other materials and equipment can usually be found around the home or school, or substitutes easily made.

The following basic information is for those readers not familiar with the use of clay or plaster. It will help in avoiding too many obvious and wasteful mistakes, though making 'mistakes' and experimenting are the best ways to discover the potential of any material.

Clay In its plastic state clay is able to retain any shape, texture or pattern given to it, and this is perhaps one reason why it has been used from earliest times for making both useful and ornamental objects. It has the added advantages of being universally obtainable, inexpensive, and easily prepared. Above all it gives satisfaction when handled. This property of being so malleable and responsive —taking the impression of any surface with which it comes into contact—makes clay the best material from which to make moulds. Sand, though useful as a mould maker, does not record subtle surfaces, while Plasticine is less responsive a material and does not provide as much tactile satisfaction as clay.

Clay, if it is bought ready prepared, usually comes from the suppliers in airtight polythene bags, and it will remain soft for a considerable time if the bags are kept closed. It can be stored in a plastic bin or similar receptacle, providing it is always covered with some damp polythene and the lid replaced. Clay that comes into contact with plaster should be kept away from clay which is going to be fired in a kiln, as even the tiniest piece of plaster can cause much damage to pottery.

To achieve a satisfactory mould the clay must be in the 'right' condition. If it is too soft and wet it is difficult to obtain a sharp and clear impression or to remove the object from the clay. If the clay is too hard and dry it is difficult to achieve a good impression without exerting a great deal of pressure.

Once the clay has been separated from the set plaster cast—and this should be done while the clay is still soft—it should be returned to the polythene bag or plastic bin, so that it can be used again. Some water sprinkled over the clay will replace any moisture absorbed by the plaster during the casting. Never let the clay harden or dry out as it means much unnecessary work separating it from the plaster cast, and then reconditioning it for future moulds.

Clay that is too wet can be dried on a plaster slab. This can be made by filling a shoe box with plaster, allowing the plaster to set, and then removing the slab by tearing away the cardboard.

If clay is too hard it should be broken into small pieces, sprinkled into a container half filled with water, and left to soak overnight. The surface water is then decanted and the very soft clay can be put on the plaster slab to dry until it is plastic enough to use.

Plaster Plaster has been used since the earliest times as a casting material, for it takes on the surface of any object with which it comes into contact; it is used extensively for duplicating objects.

There are many types and grades of plaster and all vary in their strength, texture, and setting time. They are all made from gypsum, which when 'roasted' or 'dehydrated' produces the characteristic powder form of plaster. When this is mixed with water it recovers the moisture it had prior to dehydration, and reverts to something like its original form—the solid gypsum. A well-known plaster is the one that takes its name from the material that is found near Paris. The reader working at home would be best advised to buy different types in small amounts and experiment with them, until the most individually satisfactory one is found. However, for work of this type in schools the most suitable is superfine potters' or dental plaster.

Plaster should always be stored in a dry place and kept in airtight waterproof containers or bags. If moisture from the atmosphere is absorbed by it in its powder form, a chemical reaction is started and the plaster goes 'off'. This means that a poor quality plaster is produced, which might not set; but even if it does it will not have much strength.

The mould A mould can be made by carving, modelling, or pressing objects into the clay, providing it is remembered that forms in the clay will be reversed in the cast. Even the first tentative marks made by the beginner can produce an encouraging and stimulating result. Often the surprise at seeing the clay mould being separated from the plaster can set one searching for objects that lend themselves to this work. This search adds an element of observation and discovery, that is both exciting and valuable. Almost any object can be used, so the possibilities of the marks made are enormous, and many people using these materials for the first time are pleasantly surprised by their own inventive use of the most unlikely objects. Figures 8 and 9 on pages 17 and 18 show a variety of easily obtainable objects and the casts made from them, and will probably suggest many things one could collect for casting.

The beginner should now perhaps attempt a cast following the instructions on page 12 using the objects that have been collected. Some objects, especially metal ones, tend to stick to clay, and cannot be removed without distorting the impression they have made, but dusting them with talcum powder before they are pressed into the clay usually prevents this happening.

Making a shallow relief or tile

Figures 2—7   Making a relief or tile

Materials and equipment needed

Plastic clay
Superfine dental or potter's plaster
Shoe box or any other strong cardboard box
Two plastic bowls or buckets, one filled with water
Thick string or cord
Objects to press into the clay
Newspaper to cover the working surfaces

Method (see figures 2—7)

1   Fill the cardboard box with a 50–75mm (2–3 in.) layer of plastic clay. Flatten and smooth the surface of the clay.
2   Press objects into the clay, removing them carefully so the impressions are not distorted.
3   When the design is completed *mix the plaster*. Half fill a plastic bowl or bucket with water. Sprinkle the plaster on to the water, lightly but fairly quickly, until an 'island' is formed. Continue shaking the plaster round the edges until it is lying just below the surface of the water. To avoid creating any bubbles while mixing, slide a hand to the bottom of the container, and quickly stir from the bottom, until a lump-free mixture is obtained.

4   Immediately pour into the cardboard box, covering the clay with a 25–50 mm (1–2 in.) layer of plaster.

5   Slap or agitate the surface of the plaster. This helps to force it into all the hollows in the clay and removes any trapped air pockets.

6   While the plaster is still soft, place a piece of string or cord just below its surface, as in figures 5 and 6, leaving an exposed loop from which the tile can later be hung.

7   Leave the plaster to set for at least thirty minutes. If left for longer, cover with polythene to keep the clay soft, as it is very difficult to separate hardened clay from the plaster cast.

8   Tear the sides of the cardboard box away to remove the clay and plaster.

9   Carefully separate the plaster from the clay, and wash the plaster block to remove any traces of clay from its surface.

10   Hang up by the exposed loop to display. Instead of using the sides of a box to contain the liquid plaster, walls of cardboard, wood or clay will be just as effective. These should be about an inch higher than the surface of the mould. Always make certain that the wall is strong enough to contain the plaster, and that there are no gaps through which it can escape.

Points to remember   Mix the plaster in clean plastic containers, preferably flexible ones as these are easiest to clean.

Cover the working surfaces and floor with newspaper. This will soak up any plaster that might be spilt.

Always add plaster to the water, never water to the powder. Avoid adding more water or plaster once the mixture has been stirred, as this weakens the final cast.

The water used should be at room temperature. If it is too cold the plaster takes much

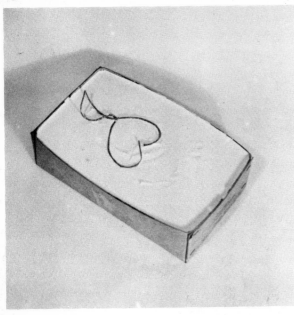

longer to set, whilst if too hot the plaster will set before there is time to pour it over the mould.

Any plaster washed down a sink will clog the pipes. Everything that has to be cleaned — hands, tools, the objects—should be washed in a bucket filled with water. Once the plaster has settled at the bottom, of the bucket, decant the water and throw away the solid plaster pieces.

Never let the clay mould harden, as it is very difficult to separate it from the plaster in that condition.

Avoid tearing the sides of the box or removing the clay before the plaster has set.

If the plaster cast breaks, the pieces can be joined with *Marvin Medium*, when they are thoroughly dry.

Any irregularities in the cast should be removed by using a *surform*. This is best done while the plaster is still damp, as it is easier and creates less dust.

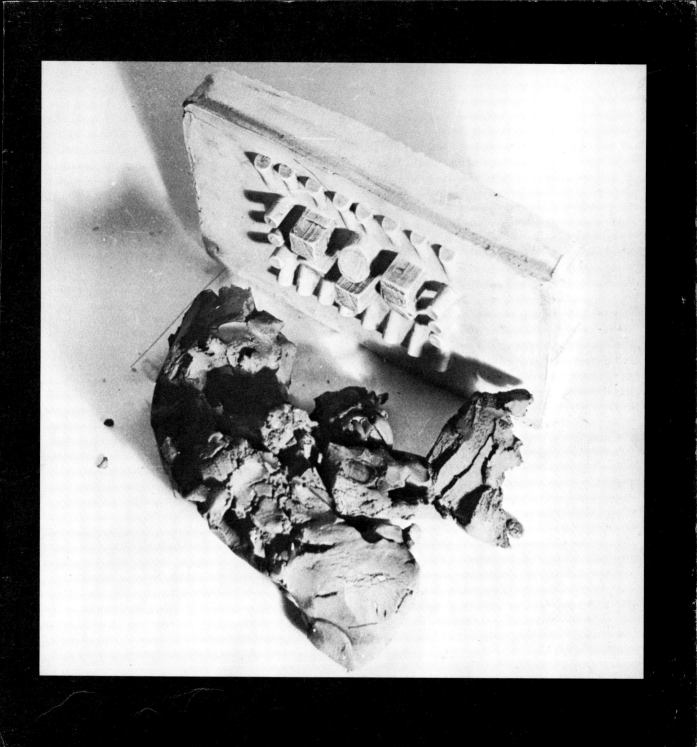

Experiments in texture and pattern making

Any object is capable of producing a great number and variety of marks, depending upon the facet, the depth, and the angle at which it is pressed into the clay. Experiments are best started by carefully and deliberately stamping with one object in regular rows at regular intervals. Then the same arrangement could be tried with another side of the object, perhaps eventually overprinting one facet with another.

Often the clarity of the organization is lost, and one needs either to choose certain parts to develop, or to return to a simple and orderly arrangement. One should be continually selecting and discriminating, and not worrying too much about spoiling an effect. The most pleasing arrangements are often the simplest.

The regularity and unity of the pattern give as much satisfaction as the rhythm that develops from the careful and systematic stamping of each impression. Besides discovering arrangements that can be incorporated into imaginative compositions, one is also learning many fundamental principles of design, for example the importance of considering the space between each impression as much as the impression itself.

Figures 10–37 show how effective results can be achieved from simple experiments with everyday objects, and they will perhaps encourage readers to experiment with the objects they have collected.

Figure 8   A selection of objects that can be used to press into clay ▶

Figure 9 A plaster cast taken from the impressions made in clay by the objects shown in figure 8

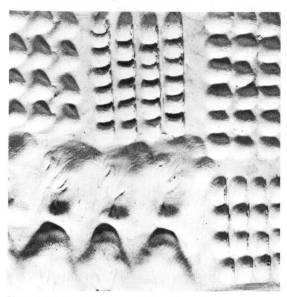
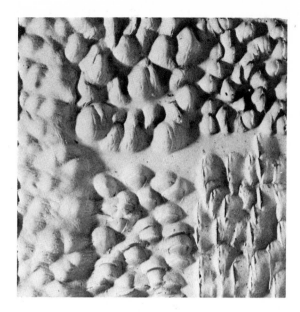

Figures 10, 11   Plaster casts taken from the impressions
made in clay by fingers and parts of the hand

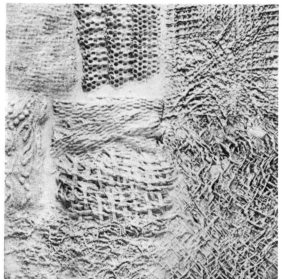
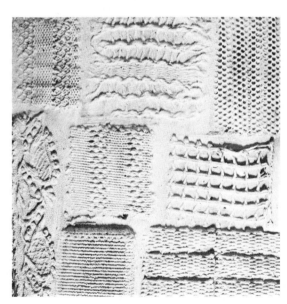

Figures 12, 13   Plaster casts taken from the impressions
made in clay by heavily textured fabrics

19

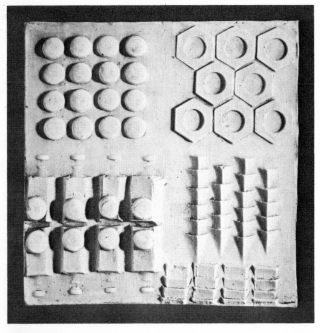
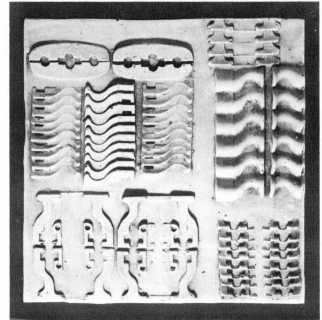
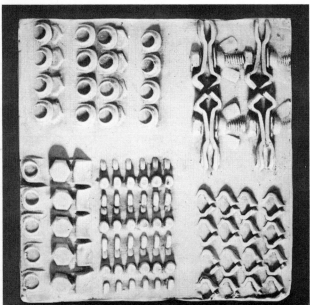
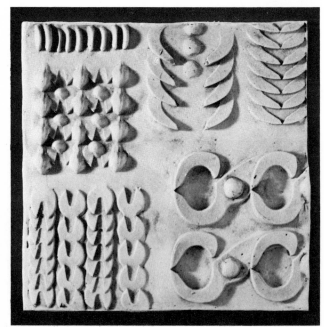

Figures 14–21 Plaster casts taken from the impressions made in clay by tools, electrical equipment, nuts and bolts and other man-made metal and plastic objects

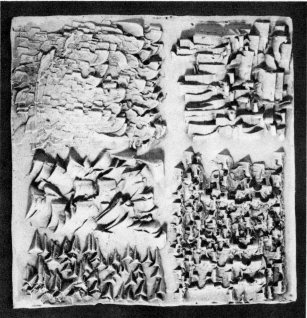
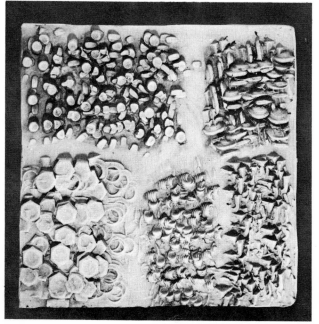

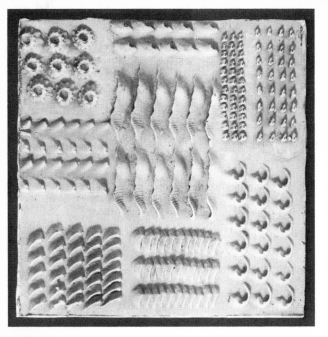
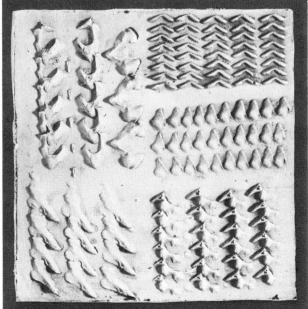
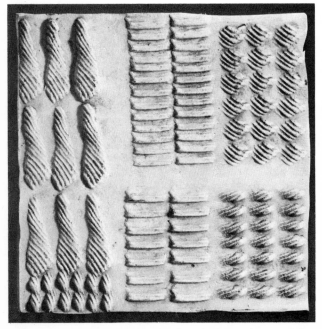
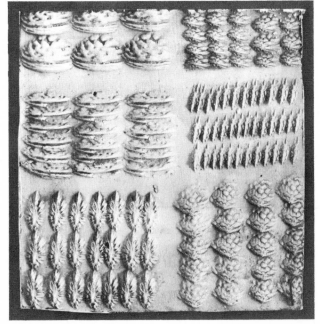

Figures 22–9   Plaster casts taken from the impressions made in
clay by shells, bones, twigs, seeds and other natural objects

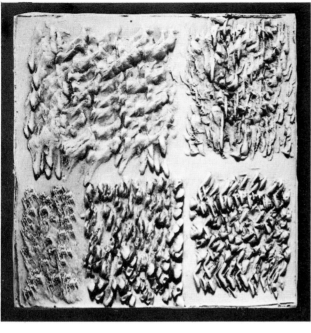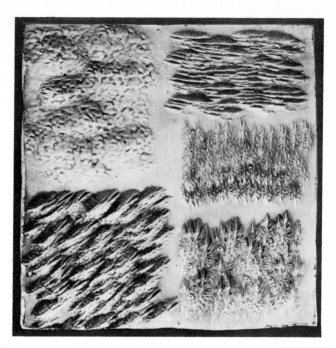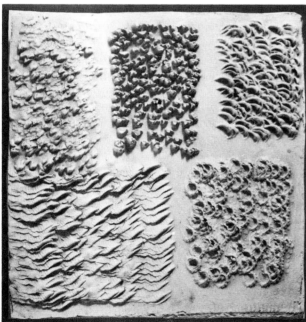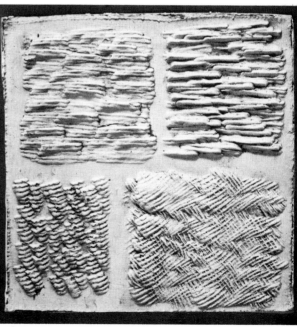

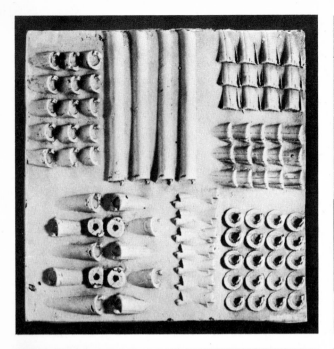
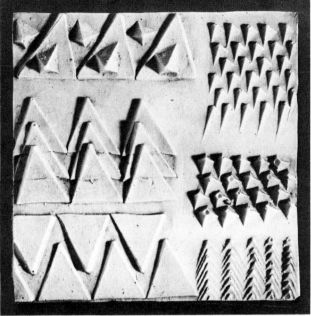
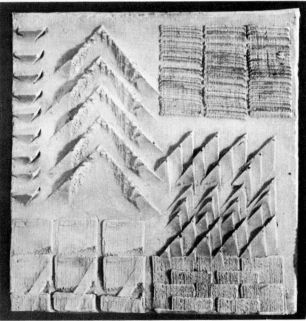
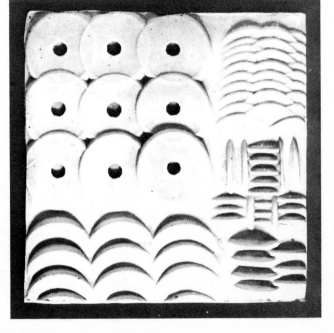

Figures 30–7   Plaster casts taken from the impressions made in
clay by pieces of wood

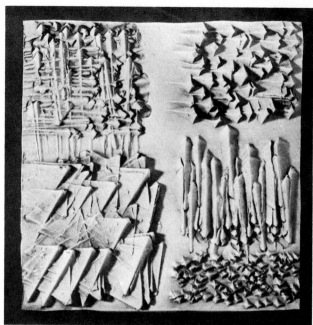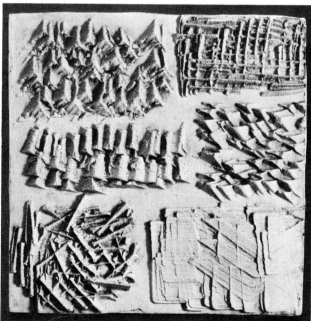

Reliefs

Figure 38   *Radial Pattern* by a student

Shallow reliefs   The reliefs illustrated in this section (figures 38–70) were made by children and students using the process described on pages 58–59. In most cases the work was based on the imaginative development of carefully observed objects. The *Robots* (figures 40, 41, 42) resulted from an examination of human forms and their translation into mechanical terms. The *Steam Locomotives* (figures 44, 45, 46), the *Traction Engine* (figure 47) and the *Motorcycles* (figures 48–51) all resulted from an interest in and careful examination of these objects. Other casts, however, developed from an interest and enjoyment of marks for their own sake. Figures 38, 39, 69 and 70 illustrate this, whilst figure 61 was the result of pure fantasy.

Figure 39   *Radial Pattern*—student ▶

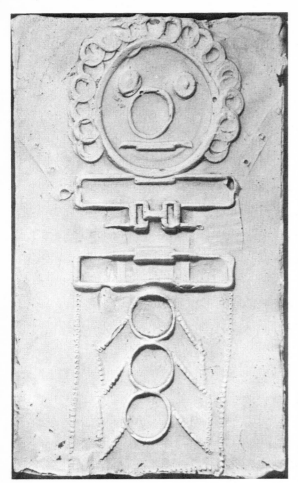

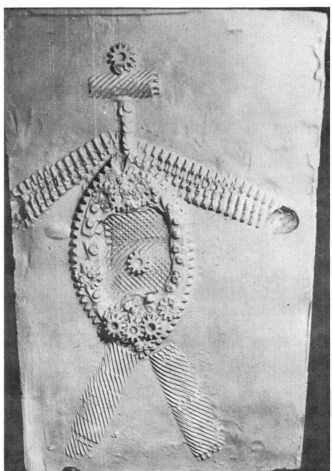

Figure 40   *Robot* by an eleven year old girl
See also colour plate between
pages 48 and 49

Figure 41   *Robot* by eleven year old Alan Gale

Figure 42   *Robot* by Jeffrey Osborne, aged eleven ▶

Figure 44   *Traction Engine* by Philip Ginn, thirteen years

◄ Figure 43   *Ocean Liner* by Janine Youngs, aged six

Figure 45 *Steam Locomotive* by Andrew Waddington, fourteen

Figure 46 *Steam Locomotive* by fourteen year old Robert Kippin

Radial Pattern. This cast, by a student, was sealed with diluted *Marvin Medium,* and silver and bronze metallic powders applied ▶ while the last application of sealer was still wet

Figure 47   *Steam Locomotive* by Trevor Risby, aged fourteen

Figure 48   *Motorcycle* by Alan Gale, eleven

Figure 49   *Rocker*
eleven year old Terry Nelson

Figure 50   *(Right) Girl on a Motorcycle*
by George Webb, aged thirteen

Figure 51   *(Opposite) Hell's Angel*
Michael   Ludlow,   aged twelve

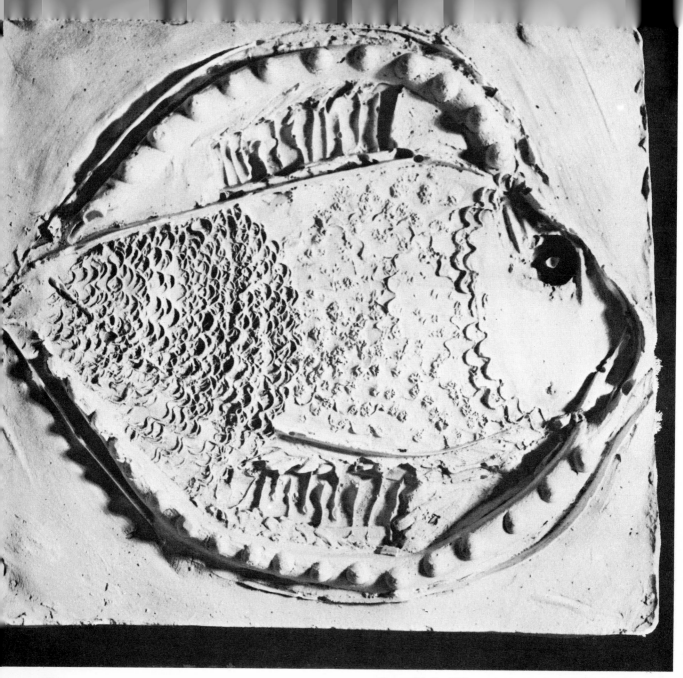

Figures 52–6   Different interpretations of *Fish* by eleven year old girls

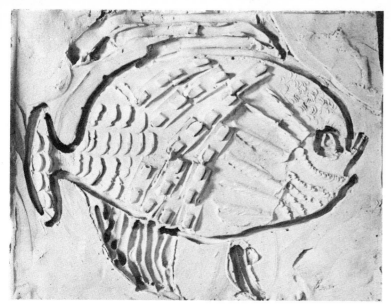

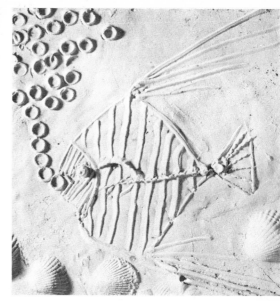

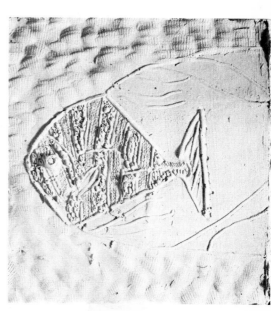

Figure 57 *Mary Queen of Scots* by Stephen Childs, twelve
See also colour plate between pages 48 and 49

Figure 59 *Egyptian Head* by Christine Bebbington, aged twelve

Figure 58 *Dolly Bird*—Angela Elwell, twelve years

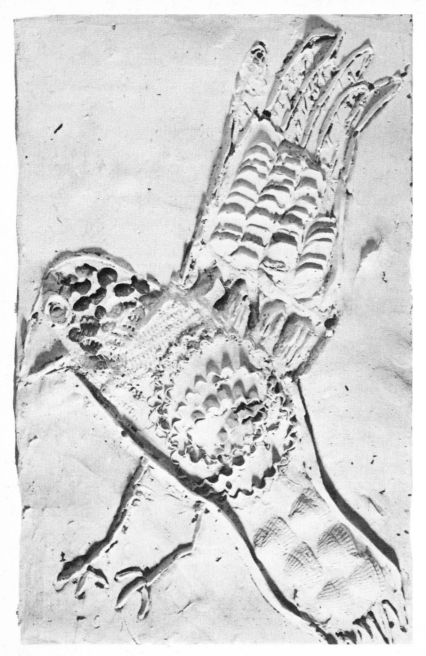

Figure 60 *Eagle* by twelve year old
Julia Cooper

Figure 61 *Figures never yet seen* ▶
Paul Lavenu, aged eleven

Figure 62   *Rhino* by Stanley Igbenabor, eleven

Figure 63   *Lion*—eleven year old Livingstone Thomas

Figure 64   *A Rainy Day* by Nichola Youngs, aged eight

Figure 65   *Home* by Sandra Griffin, eleven ▶

Figure 66   *Traffic Jam*—boy, fifteen years

Figure 67   *World War II* by a fifteen year old boy

Figures 66—8 show reliefs which were made by pressing toy soldiers, cars and animals into clay and then casting from the impressions

46

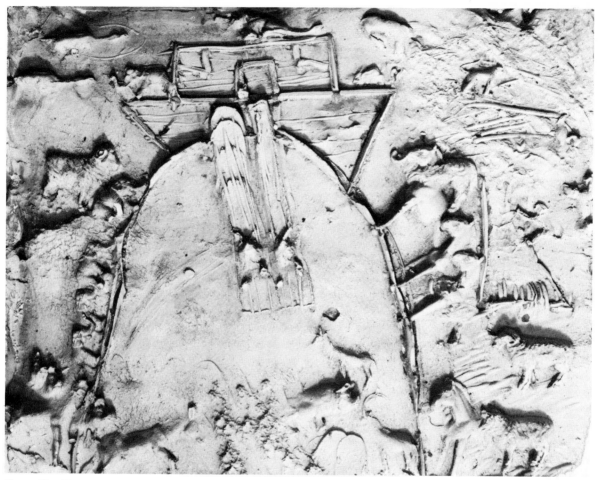

Figure 68 *The Animals Entering the Ark* by Steven Walters,
eleven years

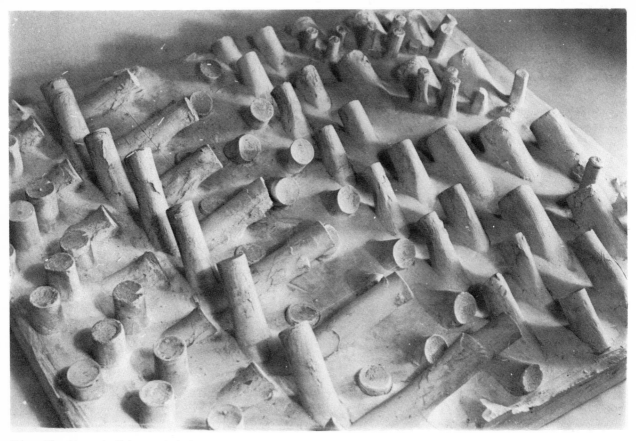

Figure 69　Alexandra Fairman, student

Overleaf

Robot by an eleven year old girl. This was sealed with diluted *Marvin Medium* and finally brushed with brown shoe polish

Mary Queen of Scots by Stephen Childs, aged twelve. This cast was painted with gouache and powder colour, after it had been sealed with a mixture of *Marvin Medium* and water

Figure 70   *Shells*—Michèle Gadsby, student

Figure 71 *Jacks, Kings and Queens*—group work by twelve year old children

Reliefs using lino blocks The impressions made by pressing a lino or wood block into clay can become the mould for a cast, producing a relief that is very different in character from one produced by any other method.

A block can be pressed into the clay more than once. This is an advantage when a large group project is being planned.

Pressing the lino block into clay and then casting from the impression produces a positive of the original block. A negative of the block can be achieved by pouring plaster directly over the block. It is interesting and valuable for children to compare positive and negative casts from the same block, and to compare the casts with prints (see also page 81).

Figure 72   Student work

Figure 74   *Head of a Robot*—student work ▶

Figure 73   *Fish*—student work

Deeper reliefs   More pronounced three-dimensional reliefs than those so far illustrated can obviously be made by pressing deeply into thicker lumps of clay. However, one often wants to obtain a cast that is not just a flat surface with projections from it, but an object that has a greater variety of forms underlying the surface decoration.

The *Head* (figure 74) was made by carving into a thick slab of clay with a wire loop to achieve the negative shapes of a face. Into these hollows mechanical objects were pressed so that the cast from it had the appearance of pieces of machinery making up the basic forms of a head.

Figure 73 was produced by carving the negative shape of a fish into a thick slab of clay, using a wire loop. Natural objects were pressed into these hollows. The cast taken from this had the basic relief forms of a fish but appeared to be made out of natural objects.

Free-standing objects

Free-standing objects can be made by carving the negative of the form required into a lump of clay. The *Car Dump* (figures 76–8) was made by using a wire loop to carve a hollow in the clay, and toy cars, lorries and tyres were then pressed into it. Plaster was poured into the hollow, and this formed the mound when the clay was removed.

Some three-dimensional objects are difficult to visualize in their negative form, however. An easier method is that of assembling individual reliefs. Two thick reliefs or tiles, of the same dimensions, glued back to back, will stand vertically, as will four tiles assembled to make the vertical sides of a 'box' (see figure 75). These units made from tiles can be stacked on one another to make tall structures.

Repeated shapes or units can be joined to make three-dimensional structures. An object, repeatedly pressed into clay at the same angle and depth can produce such a unit, when the hollow is filled with plaster. The structures on pages 58 to 61 were constructed from units cast from clay, which were then thoroughly dried, sealed with a mixture of equal parts of water and *Marvin Medium*, and then glued together with full-strength *Marvin Medium*.

Free-standing structures can also be made by lining the four vertical sides of a cardboard box with clay tiles, with their decorated surfaces facing the centre of the box (see figure 85). When plaster is poured between the tiles it produces a solid plaster shape with four decorated vertical sides. If a cardboard tube is placed in the middle of the box prior to pouring in the plaster, a solid shape with a hole through it is produced. Many such shapes can be threaded over a broom handle and fixed to a firm base, making a 'totem pole' like structure (figure 86).

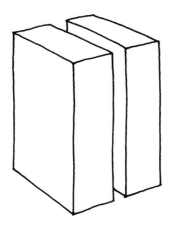

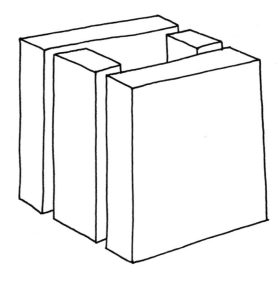

Figure 75   Ways of assembling tiles or reliefs into free standing
structures

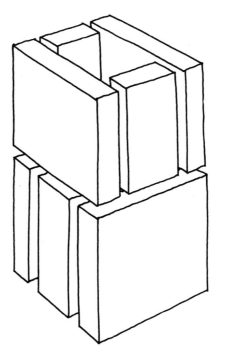

Figure 76   *Car Dump*—work of a fifteen year old boy

Figure 77, 78   Two other views of *Car Dump* ▶

57

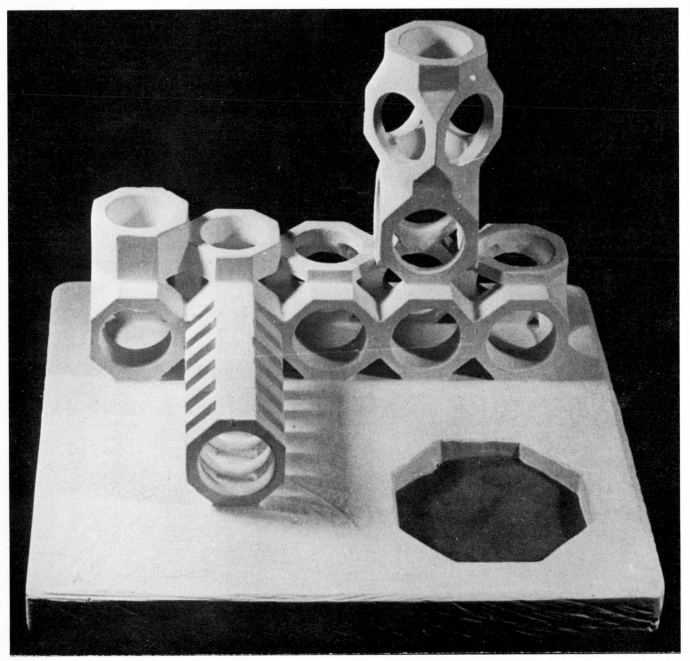

58

Figure 79 Model for a children's playground. The units were cast individually from simple clay moulds, and when dry were assembled on a plaster base. Nicos Moshatos, student

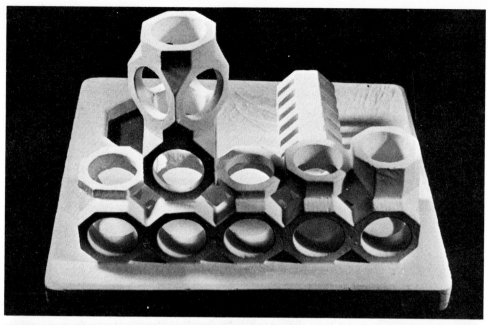

Figures 80, 81   Two views of the model shown in figure 79

Figure 82 Units made from pressing a polystyrene sphere half way into clay, and then pressing the handle of a knife into this hollow. The cast from this produced the unit shown on the right and joined together made the unit on the left

Figures 83, 84 Constructions made from the units shown in Figure 82

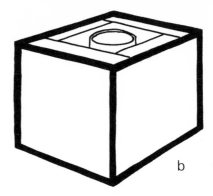

Figures 85a and b   Making a plaster block with a hole through the middle

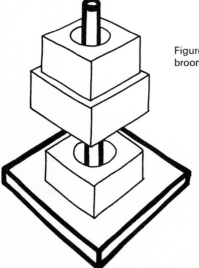

Figure 86   Displaying blocks by threading them over a mounted broom handle

Figure 87   A plaster block. The decorated sides were made by pressing children's plastic numbers and letters into clay slabs. ► These were assembled as shown in figure 85

Bricks

If a cardboard shoe box is filled to the top with liquid plaster, and the sides and base removed when the plaster has set, a plaster shape is left which is essentially that of a brick. If clay shapes which are higher than the sides of the box are placed inside the box before the liquid plaster is poured into it, a plaster brick with holes in it is produced when the clay is removed.

Clay laid in the box can consist of random scraps or carefully considered shapes. Cubes, cylinders or other geometric shapes that have been cut and the pieces moved apart can provide negatives that are particularly effective for these bricks (figures 88, 90, 91, 92, 93).

The clay for this type of work needs to be stiffer if it is to retain its shape when it is cut. Smaller clay shapes tend to float when the liquid plaster is poured around them. If this happens a weight should be rested on them. Avoid intricate clay shapes as they are difficult to remove from the plaster.

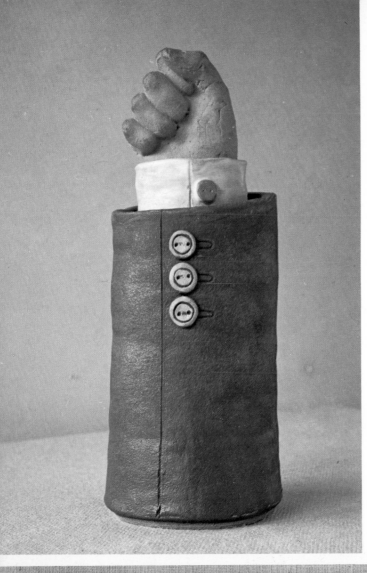

Fist and *Break-Through* by Kate Chamberlayne, a student, show how the casting processes suggested in this book can be used in conjunction with traditional ceramic techniques

In *Fist* the sleeves were made from clay slabs bent into cylindrical forms which were decorated with seams and buttons. The fist was taken from a simple two piece mould of a hand, but it was cast in clay rather than in plaster, as it had to be fired and glazed to make it a functional object — the fist was a lid to the cylindrical container or sleeve

The relief *Break-Through* began with impressions of a clenched fist in clay. The plaster casts were taken from these impressions into six soft clay slabs until they progressively distorted and at times broke through the surface of the clay. When the clay was stiffer, the plaster casts were carefully removed making certain that no plaster was left behind. The clay sections were then fired and glazed in the traditional way. Finally the plaster fists were placed in position before the clay pieces were glued onto the board for display

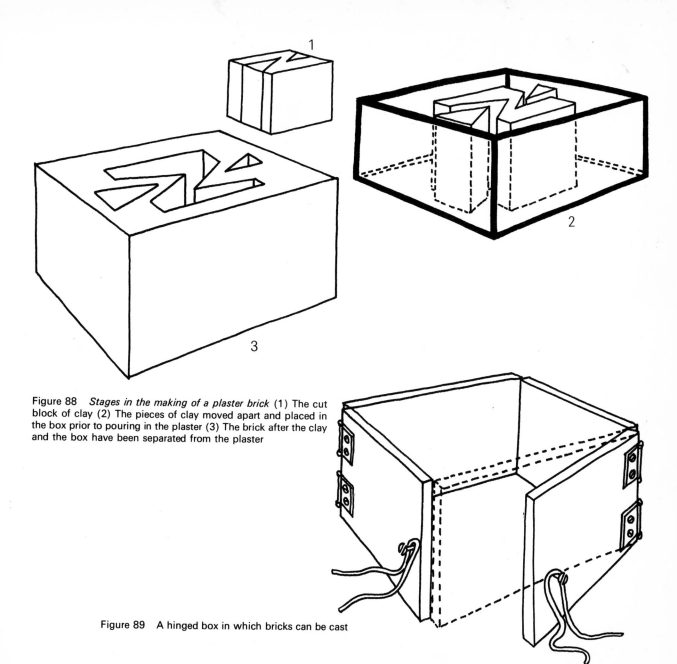

Figure 88   *Stages in the making of a plaster brick* (1) The cut block of clay (2) The pieces of clay moved apart and placed in the box prior to pouring in the plaster (3) The brick after the clay and the box have been separated from the plaster

Figure 89   A hinged box in which bricks can be cast

If a room divider or wall is being made, it is best assembled from individual bricks that are of the same dimensions. This is obviously done by using cardboard boxes of the same size, or by using a hinged box to cast each brick (figure 89).

Bricks that are not steady when stacked on top of other bricks should be surformed while they are still damp.

Figures 90–3   Bricks

Casts from the environment

The environment is an inevitable part of our visual experience, but unfortunately many beautiful and interesting objects go unnoticed because of the superficial way in which we look around us. Recording parts of it can perhaps lead to a more penetrating observation of our surroundings, as it not only focuses our vision but also our tactile senses on things we all too often pass by. Using a sketch book or camera are ways of recording what we see, but for those who feel unable or unwilling to use either, casting is a good way of recording things in order to study them.

The advantage of this process is that parts of large immovable objects can be cast, then examined at ease in the home or classroom. Careful observation of casts taken from the ornamentation and decoration on buildings, park benches, manhole covers, gates, doors, street lamps, and many other man-made objects, can lead to discussions and projects on their design and manufacture. Casts taken from natural objects develop an awareness of the subtlety of form, pattern and texture to be found in them (figures 94–111).

The impressions taken from objects in the environment should be taken home or back to the classroom for casting, if possible, rather than attempting to do so *in situ.*

The materials and equipment needed are:
Clay that is rolled out and is ready to use
A strong cardboard or wooden box, with a lid, in which to carry the clay
Thin polythene in which to wrap the clay
A soft brush, and talcum powder to dust on to metal and other surfaces that tend to stick to clay
A large damp sponge to remove any clay or talcum powder left on the surface from which the impression has been taken

68

69

Figure 99   Letter box

Figure 100   Head above the entrance to a law court

Figure 102   Stand for iron

Figure 101   Moulding on a door

75

Figures 103—5   Moulding on fireplaces

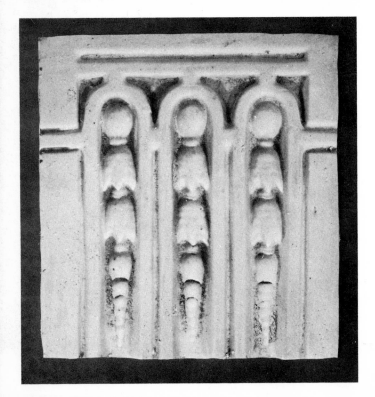

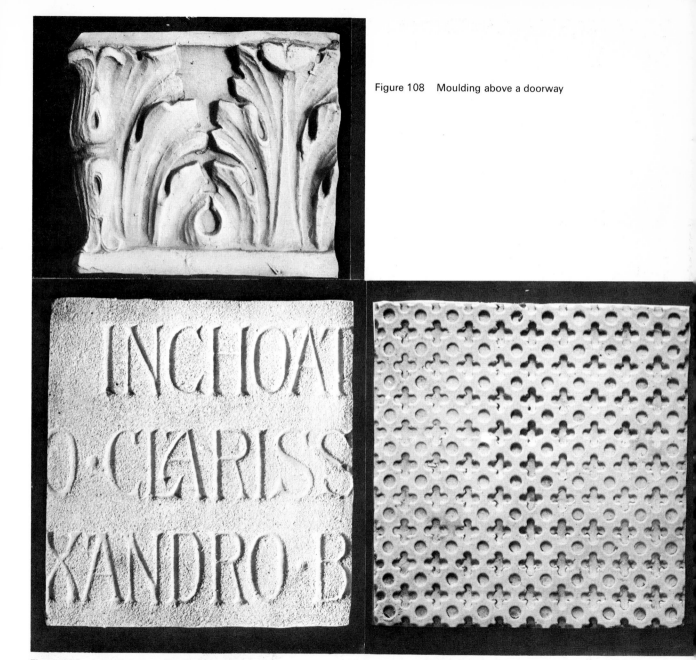

Figure 108   Moulding above a doorway

Figure 106   Lettering on a church wall

Figure 107   Garden seat

77

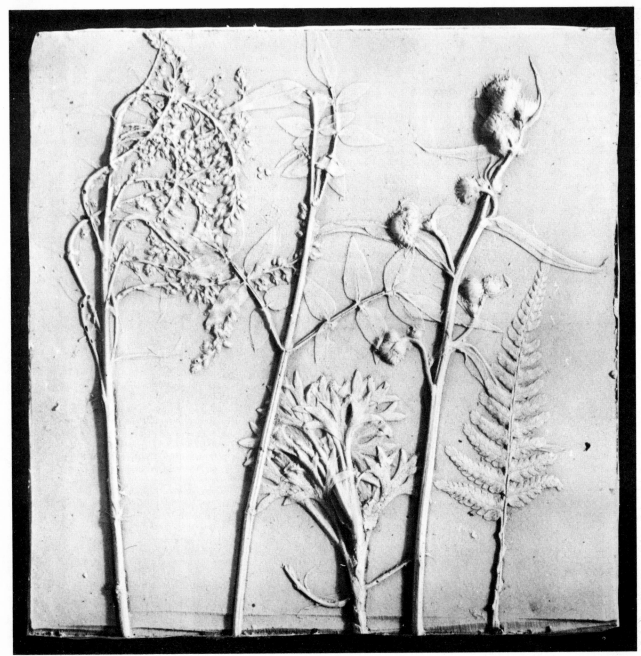

Figures 109, 110   Plant forms

Figure 111   Gravestone

Positive and negative casts

A plaster replica of the negative mould can be made by casting from any positive plaster cast, providing it has no undercutting on its surface.

The positive cast should be painted with two or three thin coats of slip—a mixture of clay and water—then more plaster poured over it. When the plaster has set, it should be put under a tap and water run over the slip, separating the two parts which should then pull apart easily.

Figure 117   Plaster negative taken from a positive plaster cast

This is a useful process if one is examining positive and negative forms with children. Sometimes the marks in the clay are more interesting than the cast from them, and this is a way of obtaining a plaster replica of the clay (figure 117).

Surface treatment and display

Surface treatment All casts should be treated with a sealer, to close the pores of the plaster object and protect the surface from accumulating dust and being easily chipped. No surface painting or colouring should be attempted until this is done. Many solutions can be used but the cheapest and the easiest is made from mixing equal parts of *Marvin Medium* with water. White Shellac, varnish and lacquer are also efficient but more expensive, and more difficult to use. Apply at least three coats of the mixture of *Marvin Medium* and water, letting each one dry before applying the next. This produces a slightly glossy finish and if it is well lighted when displayed, it accentuates even the most subtle of surfaces.

However, many people prefer to cover what they feel is the starkness of the white plaster, with all-over colouring. A most popular finish can be obtained by sealing the cast in the usual way, and while the last application is still wet, shaking on some metallic powder. These finishes are effective, though they are perhaps too expensive for large-scale use in schools, and often the cast loses the quality of the plaster and takes on the look of metal.

A cheaper way of achieving an all-over colour is by mixing powder colour with *Marvin Medium* and water, applying this mixture after the cast has been sealed. Another method is to add powder colour to the water which is going to be used to mix dry plaster for casting.

Casts can also be painted in a more direct manner as one would paint on to paper, and though the results can be most interesting, the indiscriminate use of intense colour does tend to destroy any subtlety of form.

There are enormous possibilities for enhancing plaster surfaces, and often cheap everyday materials such as shoe polish, inks, crayons, and household paints and sprays are most effective.

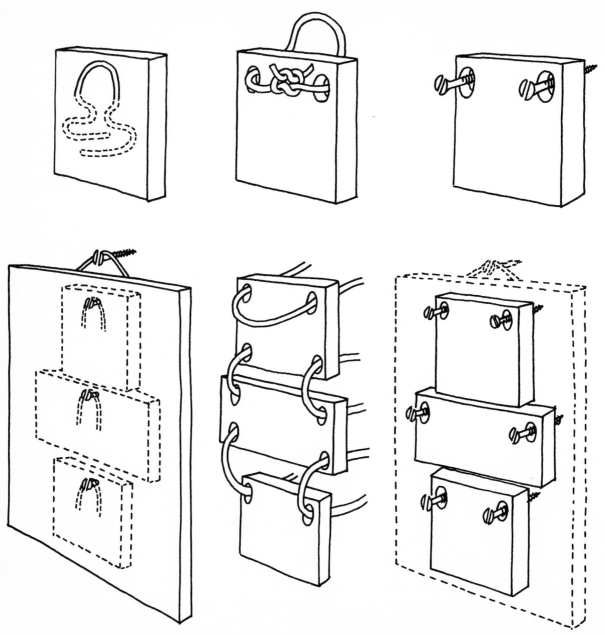

Display The way in which casts are mounted and arranged, and the surfaces on which they are placed should be as important as the making of them, and their surface treatment. With children this should provide the basis of a valuable investigation into simple display processes.

Between pouring the liquid plaster over the clay mould and the plaster setting usually leaves just enough time to place a piece of string or cord into the plaster (see figure 5). The short exposed piece will act as a loop on which to hang the cast. The string in the plaster should always be curved or bent and the two ends tied together, or large knots tied in it, otherwise it will easily pull out of the plaster cast. Too long a loop will show above the cast when it is hung. If the plaster sets before one has a chance to place the string into it, two holes can be made with a power drill when the cast is dry. String, looped through these holes and with the ends tied, can be used to hang the cast.

As shown in figure 112 individual tiles fitted with string loops can be hung from nails or screws fixed to a wall, while a tile with two holes can be hung by nails. Reliefs or tiles making up a group panel can be hung close together from nails or screws, or they can be tied together. A broom handle or thick piece of wood, fixed to a firm base, can be used to support a group of tiles by threading their string loops over and behind the wood.

The surface on which the casts will be displayed needs to be carefully chosen, in order to show them in the best possible way; and the colour and texture of the background should be related to the surface treatment of the cast. The selection of materials for the background is a valuable and interesting exercise in relating colours and textures. There are no hard and fast rules or solutions, but hessians seem to be a most satisfactory surface on which to mount casts, for their texture contrasts well with plaster surfaces, and the wide range of colours available can be used to show off brightly painted, metallic, or plain sealed plaster casts.

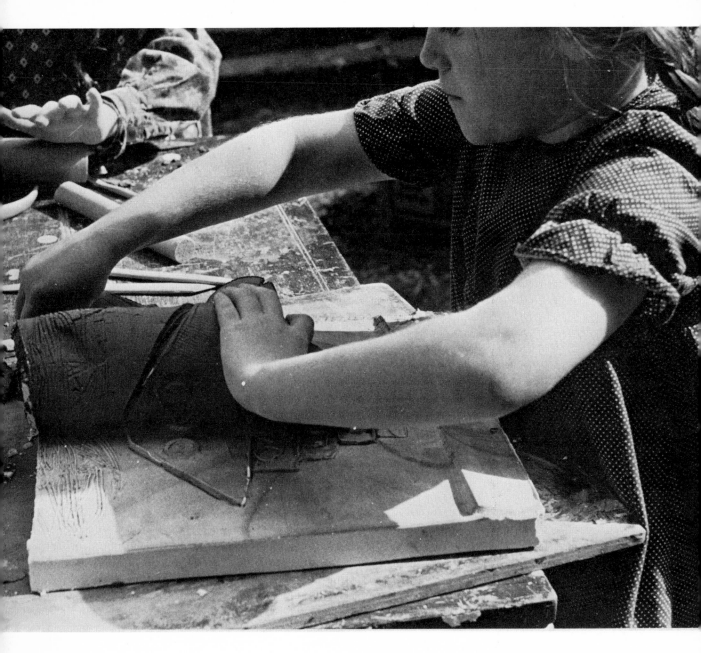

Working with children

Clay plays a valuable part in the school curriculum, both as a material for creative expression, and as a means for children to learn about the world in which we live.

However, not all teachers are able, or wish, to make every stage in the production of a ceramic object available to the children they teach. If a kiln is not readily available, clay, in the primary school, is too often limited to its use as a modelling material, and the equally important firing and glazing processes are neglected. Clay objects are made, painted with powder colours, varnished and left to harden in the classroom. They are easily broken when handled, and this often frustrates children who wish to take their clay objects home or have them displayed around the school.

If it is not possible to obtain a small electric kiln, or even to make a very simple sawdust, wood, or coal firing one—an activity children of all ages find fascinating and which provides the basis for much valuable learning—then the processes in this book show a way of obtaining durable plaster casts or replicas of the clay objects made by the children.

This work is certainly more educationally beneficial than resorting to the expensive synthetic 'clays' that are now available. These 'self hardening' clays do not require firing, or the use of glaze, and consequently do not give children an understanding of traditional and contemporary methods of producing clay objects. The type of casting suggested in this book, however, continues to explore the possibilities of using raw clay, producing objects that essentially have the quality of clay while being more permanent than unfired ones, and it also introduces the added interest of using another material—plaster.

Plaster casting is not merely a substitute for firing clay—it is a valuable and creative form of expression in its own right, and a means of discovering much about the casting process that is used for making the majority of objects in everyday use. Casting has been universally used since prehistoric times as a method of manufacturing objects, without the processes having changed much over the centuries. New materials have brought about variations, but essentially it is still *the* method

of producing a positive form from a negative mould.

Many materials can be used for taking casts. Some materials, like cements, plastics, and metals can make casting a complicated process as they need special conditions and skilful attention, which is not always possible in schools. Plaster has many advantages over other casting materials when used in schools. It does not need a separator when used with plastic clay; it is cheap and easily available; it is prepared safely by young children, without special equipment; it is quick setting so children are not frustrated by having to wait too long to see the results; and the work can be discussed and evaluated while it is still fresh in their minds.

Plaster casting from clay is an exciting way of introducing and developing three-dimensional work in schools. It is a natural extension of two-dimensional work, as very young children often draw into flat slabs of clay (and these, when cast, produce three-dimensional marks). It is a natural way of developing an awareness of pattern and texture. Marks made in clay are reversed when cast so this activity can lead to a study of positive and negative forms. Children are also fascinated by the 'magic' of plaster—its change from a liquid to a solid and the way it gives off heat as it is setting.

It would be wrong for teachers to force repetitious pattern and texture making on children before they are naturally ready for it. Very young children usually like to draw into clay, or just enjoy squeezing, hitting and generally manipulating it. Some only enjoy feeling the heat generated by the setting plaster. The value should rest on the initial exploration of the clay and plaster, and the pleasure and fascination of using these materials.

Children's initial interest in pattern and texture usually shows itself by the appearance of more surface detail in their drawing, painting and modelling. They will, at this stage, enjoy the discipline of pattern making (an activity that can often initially be linked with counting) and the satisfaction gained from the repetition of a simple shape in a larger design. Children can also be encouraged to collect patterns and textural samples from the environment. Later they could use the clay moulds to obtain casts of varying depths, and generally the work will move towards a more conscious use and development of the three dimensions. Perhaps children could be encouraged to assemble units into three-dimensional patterns—making walls and room dividers by organizing the bricks they have cast, for instance. Soon the 'working' of objects will be thought out: robots will have joints or wheels so they can be mobile; and toy soldiers, cars, and animals could perhaps be assembled to make a social statement—a comment on war, pollution or other problems.

These broad observations are by no means the only way in which children develop or respond to these materials; they are merely indications of the creative development possible for children using these processes and materials. Often a child will be found enjoying the discipline of repetitious pattern making, while soon after his energy will be directed to a wild and imaginative juxtaposition of found objects, or a sophisticated unit construction. The work suggested is suited to all ages, abilities and temperaments.

How does one start? Perhaps by taking a bag of clay into the school playground, spreading it on some polythene sheeting and encouraging young children to enjoy making marks in it. The children can be encouraged to compare and talk about the marks being made. When a sufficient variety and number have been achieved, one child could mix the plaster, under careful supervision, and pour it over the clay. The surprise and interest aroused by seeing the results will encourage children to collect other objects that can be used for future individual and group creative work.

Whichever way this work is introduced the important exploratory stages, when children are discovering the nature and possibilities of the materials, should not be cut short. Pressure of many sorts often makes teachers and children move too quickly to 'acceptable' objects for display. While being involved in exploring the materials, children will be discovering for themselves how they can be used for their individual expression. Objects they find for themselves will also suggest many possibilities. Strict instructions need only be given on the mixing of the plaster, the making of 'walls' to contain it, and the clearing up.

However, the work must be a planned programme, not an isolated technique just to provide variety. The detailed observation of casts taken from the environment can help children to be discriminating about what they see and feel, and will perhaps encourage them to surround themselves with textures, patterns and objects that they find pleasing. Group projects can encourage children to work together, each child contributing a valuable part to a large finished product. Casting from clay can be a process by which full use of the imagination and careful observation can be used by children of all ages and abilities, and can involve them in new types of thinking, new disciplines and new materials reacting and being used in new ways and opening up new types of creative work and learning.

It is up to individual teachers to create the environment and atmosphere in which they and their children can work with ease; and this is especially true of how they select, use and develop the processes suggested in this book. Nevertheless there are some points to remember when plaster casting in schools:

1   Cover working areas and floors with newspaper, and if any plaster gets on to the floor, let it dry and then scrape it off. Using a wet mop on spilt plaster only helps to spread the mess.

2   Never use the sink for washing plaster off anything, as this will certainly clog the pipes. Instead have a bucket filled with water in which to wash everything.

3   Until children are familiar with mixing and using plaster, it is advisable for only one child, under careful supervision, to mix larger batches of plaster which can then be used by all the others.

4   Children are always very eager to see the cast separated from the clay, and many fine pieces are spoilt by impatience. If possible the plaster should be poured into the mould just before a break or lunch. When the children return the plaster will have had time to set.

5   Encourage the proper care of the objects that are used to press into the clay. They should be cleaned before being returned to clearly labelled boxes. If displays are made of these

Figure 118   Janine mixing plaster

objects, children might be encouraged to bring
in others to add to the collection. This is all
valuable training for children and encourages
a proper respect for the materials and tools
they use.

Bibliography

Books on plaster and sculpture
Practical Sculpture, Robert Dawson, Studio Vista London, Viking Press New York
Creating with Plaster, Dona Z. Meilach, Blandford London, Reilly and Lee Chicago
The Technique of Casting for Sculpture, John W. Mills, Batsford London, Van Nostrand Reinhold New York
Plaster Casting for the Student Sculptor, Victor H. Wager, Alec Tiranti London, Sculpture House New York
Sculpture in Ceramic, Fred Meyer, Watson-Guptill New York

Books on Clay
A Handbook of Pottery, Emmanuel Cooper, Longmans London, St Martin's Press New York
Creative Clay Craft, Ernst Röttger, Batsford London, Van Nostrand Reinhold New York
Experimenting with Pottery, David Green, Faber London
Pottery: Materials and Techniques, David Green, Faber London
Making Pottery without a Wheel: Texture and Form in Clay, Ball Charlton and Janice Lovoos, Van Nostrand Reinhold New York
Ceramics—a Potter's Handbook, Glenn C. Nelson, Holt, Rinehart and Winston New York
Clay and Glazes for the Potter, Daniel Rhodes, Greenberg New York
Fun with Clay, Isolde Schmitt-Menzel. Batsford London, Van Nostrand Reinhold New York
The Technique of Pottery, Dora M. Billington, Batsford London
Clay Modelling, Lothar Kampmann, Batsford London, Van Nostrand Reinhold New York
Pottery Glazes, David Green, Watson-Guptill New York
The Technique of Handbuilt Pottery, Mollie Winterburn, Watson-Guptill New York

Books on design and education
Introducing Pattern—its Development and Application, Dennis Palmer, Batsford London, Watson-Guptill New York
Junior School Art, Kenneth Jameson, Studio Vista London, Van Nostrand Reinhold New York
Ideas for Art Teachers, Peter Gooch, Batsford London, Van Nostrand Reinhold New York

Suppliers

Great Britain

Clay   Plastic clay packed in ½ cwt polythene bags

Plaster   Cwt bags of superfine potter's or dental plaster

Tools and Equipment   Rolling pins, clay cutters, knives, plastic buckets and bowls, polythene sheeting
E. J. Arnold (School Suppliers), Butterley Street, Leeds LS10 1AX
Atkins Ltd, Stewarts Lane Goods Depot, Rule Street, London SW8 (plaster only)
English China Clay, 14 High Cross Street, St Austell, Cornwall
Fulham Pottery, 210 New Kings Road, London SW6
Moira Pottery Co Ltd, Moira, Near Burton-on-Trent (clay only)
Pike Brothers, Wareham, Dorset
Podmore and Sons Ltd, Shelton, Stoke-on-Trent, Staffs
Watts, Blake and Bearn Ltd, Newton Abbot, Devon
Wengers Ltd, Etruria, Stoke-on-Trent, ST4 7BQ

Small amounts of dental plaster may also be obtained from local chemists or builder's merchants
Most equipment is also available from local hardware stores

Metallic powders
Alec Tiranti Ltd, 72 Charlotte Street, London W1

Metallic paste and powder colour
George Rowney and Co Ltd, PO Box 10, Bracknell Berkshire, RG12 4ST
Winsor and Newton, Wealdstone, Harrow, HAS 5RH
and from local art suppliers

Marvin Medium
Margros Ltd, Woking, Surrey
and from local art suppliers

Suppliers

USA

Most large art supply stores carry modeling clay and casting plaster. The following suppliers specialize in sculpture materials and will send a catalog upon request.

Sculpture Associates Ltd, 114 East 25 Street, New York, NY 10010

Sculpture House, 38 East 30 Street, New York, NY 10016

Sculpture Services Inc, 9 East 19 Street, New York, NY 10003